EVEN STILL.
PROBABLY FOREVER.

or: Subtle Electric Fire

The Third Collection of "Poems" by

Isaiah M. Williams

A Zinger Media Group Book
Published by Zinger Media Group of RocketPad LLC

Copyright © 2018 by Isaiah M. Williams

All rights reserved. No part of this publication may be reproduced, stored in any form of retrieval system, or transmitted in any form or by any means electronic, mechanical, photocopying, recording or otherwise without the express written permission of the publisher.

Zinger Publications and Zinger Media Group are trademarks of RocketPad LLC.

Printed in the United States of America

ISBN 978-0-692-17412-8

Published for print and e-book distribution by:
Zinger Media Group – A RocketPad LLC Company
Cleveland, Ohio

ALSO BY ISAIAH M. WILLIAMS

Eclecticism (2013)
Selcouth Clishmaclaver or: Dancing with Strangers and Their Friends (2015)
Grasshopper: The Movie (2015)

EVEN STILL. PROBABLY FOREVER.

For the matches.

"Strike the match and get the flame."
—Unknown

Intro or: It's Cool	16
Iron Man or: Self-Fulfilling Prophecy	18
The F-Up	22
Enough	26
If Only I Was of Kenya	30
A Few Tips	32
New Rules	36
For Once	38
On the Hook	40
I Miss	44
Layla	46
Cryptically True	54
Sauced or: Aha Moment	56
Flight Delay	58
Confusion or Never Ever	60
Optimist	62
Muse, Not Mary	64
Two Words: Four Words	66
You Never Told Me	70
In Session	72
Continuum	74
Two Ears, One Mouth	76
Faustus	78
Next	80
Perspective	82
24 Maybe?	84
Screwdriver, Heavy Vodka	86
M & M	88

Colin Firth 90

Here In This Bed with You 92

Uh Huh, Right. 94

Miss Fame 96

Your Swan Song.. 98

Laugh Into My Lips 100

If I'm Being Honest.. 102

You Tell Me What It Is 104

Generation or: Do I? 106

The Break Up 108

Started as A Hello, Delivered as A Goodbye or: Even Still, Probably Forever, E... 110

part one: loading

INTRO OR: IT'S COOL

Welcome to the formative age of progress,
One in which you'll yell,
"OK Computer," but it will never
Be loud enough.

Welcome to the rest of your life,
A time you'll spend relying on
The possibility of outer space,
Where you send all of your karma,
Hoping that one day the universe
Will buck the fuck up and return it home.

Welcome to when you will explore what
Lies below your own standards and values.

Here you will learn this messed up world,
And you will very quickly forget
Your mother's fantastical decree that
Her baby was made to be great.

Welcome to the realization that
The world does in fact spin without you,
But for all you know, it could all
Stop without you around.

Welcome to an age of false voice
And a place of ruthless attention to detail,
An age you'd never thought you'd buy into,
Given your guilty distaste for all things common.

IRON MAN OR: SELF-FULFILLING PROPHECY

Though you pretend to understand
why they will not hide for you,

you cannot escape this feeling that
perhaps their progressivism has here

shown itself to be the opposite,
a lack of clarity on your position,

and what you have to lose
in this whole thing.

When you met them, you warned
them of the destruction that was

to come in the world because
Trump had just become President

and you weren't quite sure
how you felt about it yet,

but the warrior in them had only
grown stronger, and as for you, well,

your negative ass just awaited the bomb.
They would hide from the coming blast

with you in short bursts, as if to
tease what it would all be like

exposed and naked under the sun,
and you found yourself growing

more and more comfortable and caring
less and less about the consequences of

what you say and do and who sees you
do and say it much like it is when

the Jim Beam finally hits you.
Whenever the relationship was due

for maintenance, you said all the right
things to each other, and would forget

about how utterly private this all was.
But as the connection grew stronger,

it became clearer that diplomacy
was not going to cut it and that

perhaps you weren't all that cool
with Trump being in office,

so you just fucking nuked it
on your own.

part two: loaded

THE F-UP

You're cornered by the memories
Of all of the shame of your youth,

And they've led you to a place
In your mind that you weren't

Exactly sure existed until now.
Shrugging it off has become your

Favorite mannerism and vulgarity
Has become the most humorous

Way to hide behind everything
You've come to hate about yourself.

Yet when you think through it in
Your head, it sounds so sad,

But you assure everyone around you,
Yourself included, that it ain't all that

Bad. C'mon, just keep smiling
And that one scientific thing you

Read about smiling actually making
You happier will become true.

But somehow you can't seem to
Shape the shame into something

Recognizable. Instead, it's a distance
You can't seem to connect,

A 5K that never seemed so long
Until you had to run it,

A mountain that never seemed so high
Until you had to scale it.

You remember the guilt you feel for
Your mother, who worked her hardest

To make up for what was her fuck up,
For bringing you along into her anguish,

For defining half of your existence for you,
And never empowering you to learn it on your own.

For forgetting to look up from work
To see that her boy had so many questions

About life and sexuality and masculinity
And what money could really do to us.

You find yourself drunk and deep into
YouTube, seeing if Ozzy Osbourne's

Voice is still the same as it used to be,
And it's not

Like you care all that much because
You weren't even born when

The pioneer of heavy metal was
Considered surely heretic,

But you can live with the fact that
Your utmost respect for something

You did not live to see
Will have to suffice for now.

ENOUGH

one
You are more of a dissolve
    what
You said that you were faded
    yes i am on a great mixture
And I said you are more of a dissolve than a fade
    why
Because you don't go dark; you turn into something else

two
You know a lot of your body can repair itself
    yes
If you get a reasonable cut, boom, healed
    right
Even your lungs, liver, brain and bones
    what
Can be brought back to life
    in a sense
But do you know what cannot
    are you about to get sentimental
Yes
    all right
The heart

three
Why isn't it enough
    why isn't what enough
Me
    you
Yes me
    you are enough
Thank you
    i hate that word
Which one
    enough
Me too
    why
Because I don't feel it

      you are enough
Why do you hate it
      because you are more than enough

four
What do you want
      i want more of you
What more can I give you
      what you have left to give
And what is that
      whatever it is, i want it

five
Ask me that again
      where do we go from here
Where is there left to go
      far away from here
Where is here
      exactly

six
Social media
      what about it
Why do you use it
      the same reason you do
To stalk ex-lovers
      ok maybe not the same reason
So then why
      to see what's going on
People never post the low points
      what
Are you happy
      maybe
Does your Instagram give a maybe vibe
      no it's a bunch of happy shit
Because no one ever posts the low points

seven
Why isn't it enough
    why isn't what enough
That you have me right now
    i don't have you right now
You have me in this moment
    yes
And that should be enough

IF ONLY I WAS OF KENYA

Ultimately I will leave,
        not you, just all of this,
    behind.

Not a thing here in this remains
        but the blissfully toxic union
        and competition of the two
        frontrunners of the Boston,

        and if leaving all of this
        behind means betting my
        last breath to sprint ahead

        will finally separate me from
        you, it will be a task all your
        own to figure out if I am

        worth catching up to.

A FEW TIPS

one
If you see her with a guy,
And you don't look like that guy,

There's not much of a chance.

two
Even every skid mark on the turnpike
Has an interesting story behind it.

three
The best lie that you can tell someone is
That you are a bad liar.

four
Don't stay quiet when
You can die young instead.

five
If you are going to ignore someone,
Make sure to ignore them on all platforms.

six
Also, if you turn around and ignore them
The way that they ignore you,

They probably won't be as annoyed
As you were.

seven
Never let yourself be murdered
By irony.

eight
I assure you that they will get
More attractive with every sip

And the same will be true
Of your ugly mug.

nine
You can unfollow and unmatch
As much as you like but

Nothing you can ever press
Will allow you to unfuck her.

ten (3/3 = 100%)
There's always that weird point
when you see three people in

the photo and then think for a
quick second about which one

she might be, but then you
notice that all three of them

are kind of hot, so you swipe
right because it won't ultimately

matter in the grander scheme of
things because she probably won't

swipe right on you anyways, whoever
of the three she might be, and also

because if she does swipe right,
statistically speaking, she's hot.

Win/win.

eleven
When you're dealing with a person
Who really enjoys being alone,

And they appreciate you and still like
To be alone,

Well,
Take the hint.

NEW RULES

one
I am a threat to my former self.
Undoubtedly
I will forgive myself in the future.
Probably not
Though I'll still get over it and laugh.
Maybe
I can't buy into this whole system.
We must

two
A woman's entire work and worth
Is only worth the amount of time,
After translated and converted to reason,
That she spent lit up on my screen.

Three
When she asked me to eat
With her in a public place,
I thought to myself for her sake,
"Maybe. Onlookers."

FOR ONCE

You find yourself thinking about subtraction
Whenever someone tells you to make a difference

Because that's the only real thing you have ever
Known to be true about yourself,

That you're good at the nothingness,
But most certainly not good at nothing.

Perhaps you are more adept at the negatives
That are possible in subtraction.

The only true thing is fiction you think
To yourself because your cynicism has

Become the only thing that keeps you out
Of the trouble that has always found you.

ON THE HOOK

one
She broke your heart once,
And how the fuck would you react

To having to try to fix something
You didn't even know existed before?

two
That girl you had for eight months,
Yeah, you met her on an app of sorts.

And you decided just as quickly as it took
You to overeagerly say yes to her face

To keep saying yes for eight months.

three
If you put a bunch of the right swipes
Out into the universe,

Much like that good karma,
You'd think they'd be returned.

four
You look around within yourself and think
That this game can't be that fucking hard

If even the biggest thumbs in the world
Somehow figure out how to play it.

five
Your face is physically lit up
When her reflection shows up in your eyes,

And you instantly run yourself through
Two distinct but certainly sure possibilities:

She's too good looking,
So she must be fake or

She's too good looking,
So why waste the karma?

No matter,
She's too good looking.

six
God fucking damn it all because
You really don't want to have to lie

About how you met her.

seven
The fact that you can only love
Each other in private

Only makes you hate
Her in public.

eight
He asks you who the hell
Exactly you think you are,

And all you can muster is,
"Apparently, the king of one-offs."

nine
You're so fed up you've gotten to the point
Where you're going to start

Dotting your t's and crossing your i's
Just for the fuck of it.

I MISS

You see her everywhere and I can't
Even imagine how that must feel.

She was goodbye since the
Very first hello.

You essentially killed yourself
To make her love you.

Changed your views, your values,
Everything molded in her image.

You shot for the moon and then
Had to empty your whole account

To pay for instead shooting out the
Window of the building above you.

Yet you hope that when this happens to her,
She doesn't miss him the way you miss her.

LAYLA

I'm afraid to hurt you because I might end up
           in one of your poems, not exactly
sure I'd be able to live that down she says.

           But, I'm not particularly sure of
what you wouldn't be able to live down, hurting
           me or being in one of my poems.

Though you know, I didn't much concern
           myself with hurting you when I
said those things that made you place your

           thumb on your temple palm on
your eyes pinky on the other temple and your
           index on your hairline. That was

your trademark, that grasp for life on your own
           head, as if to stop your brain
from falling out of the front of your skull—

           the sound you made when I
caused this sounded like you were indeed losing
           your brain. Though you were the

one who'd say it was I who lost my brain when
           I talked to you how I chose to.
There was this one particular night, I'm not sure

           if you remember, but it started
off just fine, with me pointing out as you lay on
           top of me that you share the same

name with one of the greatest love songs ever,
           and you said by who and I said
by Clapton and you said who's Clapton and I

    said who doesn't know Clapton
and you said apparently me and I got to that point
    where I really just had to ruin a night

I knew before now you'd cherish with a great
    opportunity to use Clapton to
civilize you because I need these types of moments

    to feel like myself and before now
I was not exactly sure if you were civilized, and before
    now I was not exactly sure I could

ever feel like myself around you, but now I am for
    sure certainly you are not and I am
for sure certainly that I cannot—I hope you still follow.

And this uncertainty was never comfortable for me,
    and actually until this day I am still
not sure what you were to me; I am only truly

    sure of how you made me feel, which
honestly was more scared than anything because I
    didn't have the slightest idea of how

to deal with what I felt, so instead I just decided
    that I would ruin your night because
the sex already gave me everything I needed then. (idiot)

    I needed to inform you that you
were the perfect example of why people hate
    people our age, but you would've

slapped me if I said some shit like that, so showing
    some restraint I just told you
that you should appreciate the artistic prowess

of people like Clapton and you
told me that you never were really that into rock
    and I told you that you should be

and you told me I don't know what you should
    and should not be into and
I told you maybe so but you need to open the

    fuck up every once in a while
and you told me to fuck off and I told you that
    pretty girls like you never know

the guitar greats and you told me to really fuck off
    and I told you that you should
simply be like every other pretty girl and just reject

    the notion that you're pretty when
I call you pretty so that I can just be right, here
    about Clapton. You really did not

like that. You quickly got off of me and quietly
    started to put your clothes on,
and somehow I had not yet realized that you

    could perhaps be fed up with my
civilizing moments like when I berated you for not
    knowing what a leitmotif was or

when you forgot when my birthday was exactly and I
    didn't quite like that—though
I was relieved that you didn't ask me to say

    when yours was—or when I
actually pulled out a dictionary to prove that you
    were wrong in calling me uptight

and that perhaps *grumpy* or simply *asshole* were the
        words you were looking for in
that moment or when I got so jealous that I saw

        you kissing someone else at a
party that I punched a hole in the wall of the party
        —didn't know I was that strong—

and then only half-jokingly blamed you for scars
        on my knuckles. Back, I try to
stop you from leaving over silly Clapton conjecture

        and I gently turn you towards me
and put on the puppy dogs—as if I could really charm
        anyone—and apparently it works

because you stay. You know, I'm not sure if you are
        the beginning of a chapter or the
ending of one, and for that matter, in which book.

        That night of the Clapton mishap
I made it all work, so much so that you ended up staying
        the night and so much so that you

ended up in one of my poems without even hurting me.
        What did hurt me though was
when my feelings got clearer so my intentions got better

        and my gaze became stronger so my
jealousy got deeper and my control got more necessary so
        my options got truer and my yelling got

louder so your face got redder and my apologies became
        more frequent so you would stay over.
And although it may never become clear to me and

you, to me or you, like in love
and like in all things, we end up being—and we
        end up with—what makes sense

for us and honestly with what perhaps made sense
        for us all along. I got tired of
seeing you cry because I watched my mom do a

        lot of that shit when I was young
and you got tired of me making you cry and not
        understanding why the hell you

were even crying. God I hated how much your
        friends hated me and I hated
the person I became when I found myself hating

        them and even hating you for
not hating them for hating me. Just so much hate.
        I don't remember what I said

in those teary times, and you probably don't even
        either, but I do remember not
understanding why you cried at logic and reason.

        And obviously by the way I put
that, I still don't understand. I'm still trying to figure
        it out. And this is precisely what

I tell myself as to why we could not end up together,
        no not because either of us was
tired of hiding and not because I was too deviant for

        you and not because I was black
and you were not and not because you were a saint
        and I was ravenous and not because

I was truffle and you were vanilla and definitely not
        because we were crazy about
each other. It's because Layla is a song about one-sided

        love, unrequited feelings of affection
and lust toward something you can't have, not necessarily
        because you don't want it or need it

or deserve it, or even not because it doesn't want
        you, but simply because it does
not make sense for you. And if I was so fucking

        smart I would've noticed that
shit from the very beginning. Alright, text me
        back when you get this.

part three: the fire ain't hot enough

CRYPTICALLY TRUE

Just because you can doesn't mean
That you have to black out

All of the good that you do and replace
Its existence with memories of bad.

You fell in love with the nighttime
Because you decided it was the only

Thing that could tolerate you.
The dawn did not welcome you

With the same open arms, but
There you were again, in love.

There isn't much shame in it either
Because your love is thwarted by

The reminder that dawn is not nighttime
And bad is not good

And love is not real at least at this point
And everything you know about yourself

Aligns with the nighttime, yet you're so
Obsequiously drawn to the sunrise of dawn.

Just close your eyes and it will be dark
Just like it is at nighttime, they whisper.

SAUCED OR: AHA MOMENT

This shit won't get published anywhere,
You say to yourself after another ale.

Everything worthy is about feminism
Or how much *he* hurt *her*.

Perhaps you're much too straightforward,
You tell yourself because there's no other

Reason this shit doesn't resonate with
People in conversation, but perhaps

That's the same reason it won't
Resonate with people in writing.

It's much too sad, or it's much too real,
Or one of those kind of positive possibilities.

There's no way this experience is special
To you; there is just no way.

Suddenly, a spark of optimism, which is of course
Stupidity's synonym but nonetheless exists,

Hits you and you hope that perhaps
The silence is the proof of the struggle.

FLIGHT DELAY

Being with her is like the feeling you get
When you arrive at the airport an hour
Early only to see that after thirty minutes
Of sitting at your gate, your flight has been
Delayed an hour, and it is pinching and
Unnerving and infuriating but no one
Can really do anything about it.
But we'll make up for it, they say,
As the flight is delayed another hour.
You've heard this song and seen this dance,
And you know that this flight will be cancelled.
But they string you along, delayed another hour
They announce, before it's delayed again.
You just wish they'd announce the cancellation
Now to ease your fucking nerves and then

They start to offer the remedies as the line
Of angry potential passengers grows.
A quasi-invitation to finally meet her parents,
And then the option to change to another flight.
Mind altering sex until you tap out,
Then a voucher to fly to another destination.
A blowjob without having to ask for it,
A hotel room when the plane is delayed overnight.
Oh shit, there's a voucher for breakfast
Tomorrow morning so maybe
This isn't all that bad.

CONFUSION OR NEVER EVER

one
Some God gave you two eyes,
And you're so fucking nosy that

You're going to use them both.

two
You were so drunk last night
That you're still drunk right now.

three
You start hating yourself for even giving
Them the opportunity to reject you.

four
And out of pure irritation you provoked her
And asked her if she was gay or bisexual,

And out of pure irritation she replied
And told you that she was both,

And now you're just confused.

five
Reached out when you were horny,
And much like grocery shopping hungry,

You should never do that.

OPTIMIST

There's a very true and odd and visceral sense
Of satisfaction when you find someone

On social media you were really digging for.
Like when you see the profile picture

And realize that it's the person you've
Been looking for all this time.

Stalking is a strong word indeed,
And you prefer to instead use the term

Interest Confirmation, as to make sure
That this person is who you thought.

I bet you she's not looking into you
Like you've been looking for her.

An optimist, though, is someone
Who says that maybe she is.

MUSE, NOT MARY

You, my friend, are a leverage miner,
constantly looking for the edge.
I don't particularly find inspiration
in the blue skies of Wyoming,
or from the intensely pointless metaphors
that make most poetry unreadable,
or in simply purifying myself in
the waters of Lake Minnetonka.
My inspiration comes from that
faint red line that indicates that
you passed, though barely passed,
that long-awaited drug test,
from when 1% of battery life lasts
just long enough to finish that email,
or the feeling of child-like safety
when the direct deposit hits on Friday.
Much like the relief a black man
feels when he passes an officer
posted up behind a row of trees,
only to look at his speedometer to
see that he is doing the speed limit
but cannot resist the certain urge
to check his rearview mirror
(oh but everyone does that – shut up)
to see if the red, white, and blue
will prove black, black, and black again.
Yes, indeed, that is where
my inspiration comes from.

TWO WORDS: FOUR WORDS

Just when you thought your God
Was going to keep you on hold

Forever, the grainy music stops,
And you find yourself feeling it:

The sensation of love,
A word you've known how to say,

But not exactly what it means.
It would be like asking you to

Define "the" for example.
You want so badly to explain it,

To define it, to name it, to label it,
To package it up, to sell it, to smoke it,

To spread it, to write it down to not forget it,
That you get fed up and decide that

Explaining this feeling is like trying
To explain words without using words.

So you ban that word from your
Vocabulary, and decide that the road

You're taking is the intellectual and
Emotional high ground because you suck.

How happy you are to see her, you explain,
How often she makes you smile,

How you miss her when she's not around,
How a text is not sufficient enough,

How her smile makes you stare, mouth open,
How her hug could reduce you to nothing at all.

Sappy shit she says.
    Real shit you say.

But do you love me she asks.
    I don't know you say.

Do you even love yourself she resigns.
    The best barbers are bald you say.

part four: somehow optimistic?

YOU NEVER TOLD ME

Did you ever stop to think
how bad I feel for saying
"No" all the time?

No, but much like the deaf,
I did not choose to split my
life into silent and soundless.

IN SESSION

You, good doctor,
self-prescribe and

medicate until you
levitate far enough

above yourself, out
of yourself as soon

as there is no class
tomorrow, though

honestly you didn't
have much class

today either. Tonight
you will dance with

the stars until you
can look down and

forget to remember
that you will at some

point have to forget
again to feel like it

is actually the weekend.

CONTINUUM

I am the elephant that tested
the Brooklyn Bridge because

there is not one over troubled
waters that I have not endured,

not one that I have been scared
to walk over, and not yet one that

has given way, cracked beneath my
large legs and lost to the gravity

pulling it towards the earth, crumbled
into itself, having lost its bearing—

crashed—to the booming waves below,

and as much as I like to think I am like
the elephant, brave and courageous,

though foolish for even taking the steps,
I have somehow never lost to gravity.

TWO EARS, ONE MOUTH

Say something
so fucked up
that I can steal
it.

Because this
truth is
stranger than
fiction shit
doesn't write
itself.

FAUSTUS

I have tried too many
times to sell my soul,
she whispers into your ear,
as a postulation for why god
and the devil certainly do not
exist, and the only thing that
comes to you in that moment,
though you probably agree,
is that perhaps her soul is
not worth very much yet.

NEXT

You know, that you were so sure
That in every story you ever read,

The hero got lonely at some point,
Missing and wanting something

They couldn't have, and so much
So that you had gotten to place

Where she fucked you up so bad
That you would get so lonely

That you would've slept in between
Her and her new lover just to be

Next to her.

PERSPECTIVE

I am for once emptying the basket
that for you in which I laid all my eggs

because it has become too heavy for me
to carry around, as I have realized now

more than ever that I really do not come
into myself, like a freshly washed car into

a garage hiding from the rain, but instead
I come out of myself like thorns from a rose

or the grease that creates acne on a teen's face.
Yet somehow it was not I who chose this order

because I took my chair and placed it on its side
and crawled onto it as if it were still upright and

as if I myself was sitting normally, and I looked
over to the crowd who sat upright and yet riskily

leaned back in their own chairs and looked at me
fiercely and told me I ought not be on the ground.

24 MAYBE?

Your older
buddy told
you, the smug
son of a bitch,
that the reason
you've been so
successful at
holding that girl
down is because
you, and she, are
at the age where
you can get away
with all that shit
because she does
not yet realize
that she is worth
more and you do
not yet realize that
you should be more.

SCREWDRIVER, HEAVY VODKA

Pour it up

strong

because you
know you need
to get one in you
before you start
to bore her.

M & M

The difference is striking.
The level of interest from

one particular group of this
fucked Earth's fucked population,

that favors such a subset,
a subset of a subset even,

so much so that it informs
the reciprocation of said favor,

and turns even the most traditional
standards of the human race,

the usual way, onto its head,
though speaking of that,

it only makes reciprocation
more probable.

But of course, still, you'll never
let yourself forget the traditional way,

right?

COLIN FIRTH

It never occurred to me
    that although you

had the most impressive
    way about you,

and impressive is a word
    reserved for actually

impressive people,
    that you were drawn

to the appeal of
    bad-assery.

Well, baby, I just want
    to remind you that

although you're an
    action star, at least

I do all my own stunts.

HERE IN THIS BED WITH YOU

No, I'm not exactly where I need to
be or where I belong for that matter,

because like Maya Angelou said,
I really belong nowhere, yet somehow

despite all the self-doubt I could
muster into existence, I am exactly
where I want to be.

Then again, while you ride up there
on your horse on a level known to

very few like me—not because I
can't reach it, but mainly because

you have yet to explain it to me—
just remember that I'm still trying
to find myself in all of this.

UH HUH, RIGHT.

You keep
drinking like
tonight
is gonna
be the last
night you'll
be drinking
for a long,
long time,
and you
keep eating
like tonight
will be the
last night
you'll be
eating like
shit for a long,
long time
because the
diet starts
tomorrow.
So tonight,
you'll finish
that handle
Because you
honestly can't
afford to buy
another one.

MISS FAME

More Popular than Jesus has its own Wikipedia page,
and much like the America of 1966,
you did not appreciate it when I said that I was a god.

If you were familiar with the history of rock and roll,
you would know that this was the comment that ended the
North American touring life of The Beatles,
but you know what,
fuck you because they ended up the most thought of band
ever.

YOUR SWAN SONG

She seemed to have caused
you to bottom out,

not in the sense that you've
hit a rock on the bottom

and will now begin to rise,
as the traditional saying

does indeed go, but
more so in the sense that

you've hit the bottom so
hard that you destroyed it

from beneath you so you
just keep on falling.

LAUGH INTO MY LIPS

Fuck you, you laugh into her lips, because she teases you because you say you're on another level among twenty-somethings because you appreciate Bowie and Knopfler and Reznor and Iommi and Dio, yet you know that it's not your appreciation for these gods that sets you apart, but instead it's that you're smart enough to use them to impress a girl that very much already loves you, and you think this to yourself as you pull more deep cuts of entertainment out of your asshole, and now you've come to how you appreciate the cinematic stylings of Bogdanovich and Miyazaki and Kubrick and even that fuck face Polanski, but she only laughs mostly because she doesn't give a fuck about your knowledge of these people but also a tad bit because she doesn't know these people, and you're not exactly sure which pisses you off more just as she asks you a question, on top of you and ready to have you, as to whether or not you actually appreciate these artists or just collect and consume them for moments like this, and this question is so disconcerting to you that you just smile devilishly, growl a bit, forget, and fuck her like you'll never see her again.

IF I'M BEING HONEST

I wish some old dude,
or otherwise wise person

would tell me why the hell
I lie

in my bed and fantasize,
if that's even the right word,   (but I think it is)

about you and he lying there,
he being what you need then,

me being as far away as possible
because I can't exactly do that,

and his fucking lips on yours,
his eyes probably closed,

because some girl in his checkered
history broke his heart like you say

I broke yours.
His gin breath seeping out of his

nose onto your entire face,
and it's as if your skin absorbs it,

and finds a new love for it,
a new place on your mental shelf

of awesome shit that you will
never forget,

and you become a little drunk on him,
but me, well, I finally fall asleep.

YOU TELL ME WHAT IT IS

I make love
to what I
will never be.

GENERATION OR: DO I?

I think it's
insanely weird
that others
constantly
associate my
generation with
the negativities
of kale and
Starbucks and
shit like that
instead of the
fact that we all
frequently joke
about wanting
to be dead.

THE BREAK UP

one
Friendly fire and lost desire
I shake my head to death.

two
Do you even remember
what it was like when
it wasn't like this?

three
Close your mouth
when you leave,
and tell me what kind
of taste I left in it.

STARTED AS A HELLO, DELIVERED AS A GOODBYE OR: EVEN STILL, PROBABLY FOREVER, E.

It is as if I did not remember
what the truth of my reality was.
It is as if the hope that has become
my crutches struggle to prop me up,
my broken Achilles.
I am a broken man.
I am a needy man.
I am broken. I need.

Love me, dammit.
Or at least love me differently.

Whenever I'm around you
it's like I'm holding my breath,
holding my words,
refraining from saying something
that will disappoint or confuse you.
I am afraid to communicate,
and I am afraid to groan,
as it might reveal what I am
trying to keep hidden.
When you leave, or I leave you,
I exhale, releasing the pent up
anger I feel toward myself
for being so foolish and expecting
too much.

Quiet now.
Take my heart (god that's fucking terrible but I feel it)
and literally hold it in your hands if you need to
while you see what I mean by it.
I will validate you,
love you like you've
never been loved before.
You're good enough for me,
and that's for sure.
All of you I suppose.
I'm waiting now,

giving my presence
to you, but you have
no idea I'm even
in the fucking room.
I love you.
I love none of what
your mother sees,
but all indeed of what I see.

I trust that
you don't love him
that way I hope you don't.
But knowing my luck,
I'll probably be disappointed.

Well I think it's pretty
much confirmed.
Him not me.
Not confirmed because
you said it but because
I say it, and I'm usually
so right about the shitty
parts of life that they should
pay me to predict it.
I'm lost, E.
I'm so lost.
Like a fucking child
wandering the forest
of a foreign nation
in a different world
of a fucked up universe
in a parallel dimension.
Love me. Tell you. Love me.

I should just tell you
the things I've always
wanted to.
That I am attracted to every

part of you,
every fiber of your being,
everything that you do
attracts me,
even the things that piss me off.
That I hate him,
hate seeing him,
hate being in the same room
as you two because you touch,
you hug, and I sit.
It's funny.
That you mean so much to me,
a man who has never cared
about anyone,
who has never loved anyone,
who has never been in love
with any one.
That I care about you,
that I love you,
that I am in love with you.

Like me. Love me.
For my soul can no longer
bear the effects of being a coward.
Forgive my pettiness of heart.
I expect. I am disappointed.
He must go away.
Or I must be assured
he is no longer to stay.
No longer.
Just give me the chance to tell you.
Give me a chance to love you.
He's everything you want and need.
Yet I don't want you to be happy
with him.
I want you to be happy with me.
So I guess until then, suffer.
Suffer

suffer
suffer until you come around.
Suffer until I fucking step up.

Sometimes I make pretend that you are mine,
and other times that you wish that were true.
And sometimes when I am near you or even
in the same room with you, I forget that
it will never be true.

I wish that knowing you was enough.
I really do.
I wish that meeting you
and cherishing you as a friend
was enough to quench
the disgustingly unquenchable thirst
that I feel to be with you,
not to fuck you even,
nor to make love,
but just be with you
and have you acknowledge
that I'm not the only one
who wants this to be
something more.

I want you internally like the
ocean wants to reach the shore,
over and over again,
reaching, but subsiding,
reaching again, but subsiding again.

I am fucking stuck between
whether or not I should
smile because you are my friend
or weep because that is
all you will ever be.

I want so badly to blame you

for feeling the way you do
about him, but as soon as
I do, I remember it is
that same irrationality that
makes me pine for you.

Here I am,
far away from you,
not geographically per say,
but far away,
thinking about you,
missing you,
sulking for you,
feeling sorry for myself,
and knowing that you
have no idea about
any of it.

To make myself feel
mildly better about
this shitty situation,
I label it a slow crawl.
A slow crawl to your warmth,
a slow crawl to the revelation
of my hiddenness that itself
is inevitable.

I think that I will always
love you.
Somehow, even, I think
that I will always be
in love with you.
Yet, it is now, in this
very moment,
that I truly,
for the first time,
do not want to.
So it is here that I must

end this charade.
For the both of us.

Only if I hadn't
Denied you the
Explanations to all this.
Trepidation I suppose.
Oh, who knows?
No more.

Just kidding.
I am still very
fucking much in love with you.
Weight I must lose.
Weight I will lose.
Mine you will be.
Yours I must be.

You used to put your head
on my shoulder,
and breathe into me,
breathe out your troubles,
breathe in my wisdom.
But now you just ask me
about what to do with guys
in whose position I wish I was.
It seems as if I breathed in all
your trouble but you seem to
have neglected all of my wisdom.
My shoulder misses you.

You don't like sappy things,
and perhaps that is why I love you.
I know that if you ever read
this poem,
they will not be met with kindness
from you,
and they will not be what makes you

fall in love with me.
And that's exactly why I need you
to fall in love with me.
Because I appreciate that disregard
for sappy shit in you.
September?

You're negative,
abrasive,
so fucking fucked up.
You're perfect for me.

One day I'll tell you;
I promise.
And you'll fall in love with me.
Well, you're already in love with me.
You just don't realize it yet   (god, I sound crazy)
because I'm hidden in this body.
September. I promise.

I'm a fucking mess.
I don't even want to be with me sometimes.
How could I expect you to?
No matter what I conjure up to say.

Rest assured that I am not
obsessed with you.
I am more obsessed with what
you represent to me:
the first girl in many years
who I found emotionally
and physically attractive
who actually paid attention to me.
Platonic attention though it was.
And therein lies my problem.

I *must* let you go.
Not because I want to.

But because this is too
One-sided for me to function.

I would drop anything to be with you.
Even still. Probably forever.

But the truth is you haven't
been the same kind of friend
to me that I've been to you.
How could you be?
The only way you could
possibly meet the expectations
of you being a good friend to me
would be to date me.
And therein lies another problem.
I created an impossible expectation.
A reality that only exists in a daydream.
I don't belong in that daydream.

I will never be happy

with just your friendship; I'm sorry to say.
I need your acknowledgement.
Hurting you is never my intention.
Maybe ending this friendship won't
hurt you as much as I think it will,
but I've been hurting ever since I met you.
I've watched the only woman I've
ever loved break down because of
another guy, who won, who beat me to you.
I've watched the only woman I've
ever loved crush on men I know
I am better than.
I've watched the only woman I've
ever loved ignore the fact that
I loved her, so that she could
Preserve our friendship.
I need peace. I need this to end.

Because as long as I'm not with
you in the way I want to be,
I can never be a true friend to you.

**I would drop anyone to be with you.
Even still. Probably forever.**

I've dreamt too often that one day
you would wake up and realize that
we were meant to be together,
and perhaps that day will come,
but as history tells us,
I'm a pretty good guesser.
So it won't come.
I can't make you love me.
This is something you can't force.

The trouble I have is that this
was so natural for me.

I can't explain why I care so much
about you, and frankly I can't explain
why I care about you at all.

I lost the weight for you.
Yeah. All 115 was motivated by 1.
I could've been perfectly content   (just kidding)
chasing chubby chasers and getting
drunk with my sad friends.
Somehow I thought my body was a cage
that kept me from dancing with you,
Arcade Fire style.
In a way it was.
I was toastered because of it.
Because, hell, I am perfect for you.
Fuck, everyone can see it.
And you're perfect for me.

But you made up your mind on fat boy,
and there's really no changing it.
I would have to meet you all over again.
                (maybe. probably not. who knows? ha.)
I can't meet you all over again.
I can't fix my teeth.
I can't fix my excess skin.
I can't fix my crippling jealousy.
I can't fix my manipulative ways.
I can't fix you.
But I don't want to.

I will leave this friendship:
knowing that I fixed a broken woman
when she was at her utter worst,
broken by a man she had no business with,
and fixed by a man who had no business fixing her;
knowing that I made you smile,
even when you didn't want to;
knowing that I gave you over
a year of the best friendship
I've ever given anyone and that
anyone has ever given you;
knowing that I wasn't good enough for you.
Please don't tell yourself
I'm too good for you.
Because that's just your psyche
trying to convince you that
you're not breaking my heart.
This will hurt.
But it's not a choice you made intentionally.
Ending this is one I made.
I need peace.
And being your friend will not bring me peace.
I'm not even sure that being your boyfriend
at this point would either anymore.
Sorry if this poem is reminiscent
of all of your other guy friends

who were also in love with you.
I can assure you of one thing though:
they were never like me.
Decipher that as you will.
I ask you only one thing:
that you don't make this
harder than it has to be.
My mind is made up,
just as yours has been
ever since you met me.

Goodbye, E.

I'm sorry that I couldn't get to you.

---

afterthoughts

this was the somehow the only poem in the book about you
    it did hurt
you more than me
    but nevertheless it remains
i would drop anything to be with you.

Even still. Probably forever.

www.ingramcontent.com/pod-product-compliance
Lightning Source LLC
Chambersburg PA
CBHW032140040426
42449CB00005B/327